TOXIC PARENTS

HOW TO PROTECT YOURSELF AND HEAL FROM THE ABUSE

Micah Stephens

©January 2022

TABLE OF CONTENTS

SECTION 1
OPENING THOUGHTS

INTRODUCTION

After beginning therapy and studying to recover from suicidal depression and chronic anxiety, I started finding out just how important your relationships are to your mental health. I learned that if you have dysfunctional relationships around you with little to no boundaries, it will either cause or at the very least perpetuate serious mental health issues, like depression, anxiety, chronic stress, eating disorders, OCD, and addictions.

After learning that the toxic relationships in my life were contributing or causing my mental health issues, I began to devote a lot of my time learning to recover from and deal with the toxic people (mostly parents) in my life, which included setting boundaries, getting over people pleasing, guilt over setting boundaries, fear of others and authority figures, and recovering from emotional abuse. But when I met and married my wife, lo and behold I realized that I married someone who also had toxic parents, so I got the "pleasure" of learning the skill of dealing with parent in-laws, and a spouse that was on a very different page than I was.

So the past 15 years, I have learning from several different counselors, have read dozens of books, but most importantly I have practiced and seen what actually works in dealing with toxic parents and in-laws, how you can find the confidence to deal with them, and heal emotionally and mentally from the abuse. A lot of my relationships got much better, others got worse and completely dissolved. Since then my mental health has gotten significantly better, there is a lot less stress in my life, and my wife and I look forward to the holidays rather than dreading them.

This is what I am going to share with you in this guide so you don't have to spend years and thousands of dollars like I did to learn all of these things. If you have toxic parents or in-laws or even decent parents or in-laws that just need to be confronted about some things, I'm positive this is going to be a big help to you.

Happy reading!

CHAPTER 1:
ARE THEY TOXIC

What exactly is a toxic parent? Various dictionaries define "toxic" as harmful or very unpleasant. Although toxic parents often won't harm us physically (though many do), their behavior can cause emotional and psychological harm. This is trickier because there is not an objective form of measurement to give us proof. However, just because there is not an official observable measurement, that does not make your feelings less real or trustworthy. Your emotions and even your body will tell you if a parent is toxic to be around. **Trust your feelings.** Ask yourself how it feels to be around your parents (or in-laws). Do you feel stressed, guilty, pressured, or devalued? Do you feel anxious before spending time with them? If so this not a good healthy relationship. And if you feel this way about them and not everyone else, chances are the issue is with their behavior and their energy not your imagination.

21 SIGNS A PARENT IS TOXIC OR NARCISSISTIC

To help you gain further clarity on whether a parent is toxic, here are 21 signs that are telltale signs (according to psychologists).

1: Feeling and acting superior to others

There is nothing wrong with having an appreciation for one's gifts, talents, and skills and have a good sense of self-worth, but toxic parents believe and act as though they are *better* and more important than others. They will act and treat others as though they are below them.

2: Lack of empathy

Toxic parents have an inability to understand or consider how their children feel. They care very little (or not at all) about other's needs and feelings. They can be completely unphased when their behavior deeply hurts their children and will keep the focus on their hurt feelings that someone else might suggest they are less than perfect.

3: Being controlling.

Control is when we try to force or make someone do something or not do something against their will. Toxic parents will do this by telling their adult children what to do, demanding from them or being pushy, and oftentimes they will use intimidation where they try to use anger to invoke a sense of fear or shame in their adult children to get them to do what they want them to, or not do what they don't want them to do.

4: Belittling others

Toxic parents often love putting their children down in a either a direct way with blatant insults, but also very often in the form of "jokes." Although sometimes we can poke a little fun at each other from time to time lightheartedly, the narcissist does this too often and goes too far, and does not care if their adult child express discomfort.

5: Disrespecting noes.

Though many of us can feel a little upset when someone says no to request, we can still treat the person with understanding, but the toxic parent cannot do this and will instead act wounded or get angry and will then try to intimidate their adult child or push them and guilt trip them to change their mind.

6: Using others

Many toxic parents see their children as pawns for their self-gratification and pleasure rather than human beings worthy or love and respect. They tend to have very high or many expectations of what others should do for them or give to them. They will use their children (both as a minor and as an adult if they can) for their own pleasure and get very frustrated when they won't cooperate.

7: Fragile egos

Toxic parents act very emotionally wounded or angry when you address an issue with their behavior. They will make it all about them and their feelings and try to make out the child confronting them or setting a boundary is the bad person or the abuser.

8: Making conversations about themselves

Toxic parents have little interest in their children unless gathering information about them is self-serving in some way. So they will turn the focus of most conversations to themselves. They might initially start a conversation by asking about you and your life, and once you start talking they will find a way to make the conversation about themselves and take up the rest of the time talking about that.

9: Being manipulative

Toxic parents will often try to control others by invoking a sense of guilt, or another negative feeling that will influence them to do what the narcissist wants. They will often act sad, hurt or lonely as a way to get others to do what they want.

10: Being critical

Toxic parents will vocalize their displeasure in other's choices either directly or indirectly (passive aggressive). Since they are so controlling and perfectionistic, they often have many negative comments to say about others.

11: Acting entitled.

Toxic parents believe they have rights to other's time, energy, resources, anything that belongs to them. This will manifest by the narcissist grabbing or taking what is yours' without asking permission. Examples might be them borrowing something without asking, walking into your house without knocking, showing up without asking, or picking up your children without asking. They have little to no boundaries because in their mind what's yours' is theirs' and what's theirs' is theirs'.

12: Being demanding

Toxic parents don't ask for what they want, they demand it. They tell others what to do instead of asking because asking would mean the other human being is equally deserving of respect, and the narcissist can't allow that.

13: Being argumentative about different view or opinions

Toxic parents love arguing with others about

different beliefs and opinions. Particularly politics and religion. The goal of the narcissist in discussing these topics is not to understand the adult child's point of view, but to control what they think. If the narcissist cannot control the adult child's opinion after some time of arguing, they will revert to insults, intimidation and humiliation.

14: Boundary crossing

When you set a boundary with a toxic parent or ask them to stop a behavior they often continue. Sometimes they will flat out refuse to stop when you ask them to stop, or they will agree to stop and then continue while pretending they forgot or claiming they don't remember doing what you are saying. Toxic parents believe they should be allowed to do whatever they want to others, and when people tell them they have a problem they see this as a violation of their deluded idea of what their rights are.

15: Gaslighting

When confronted about an issue, toxic parents will try to make the victim of their disrespect or abuse doubt their memory or perception. They might insinuate the person is being overly sensitive. They might play dumb and say they don't remember. Or they might flat-out lie and say what they said or did never happened. Although parent can forget things from time to time, with narcissists you will find they have a habit of not remembering things.

16: Demanding forgiveness, trust and/or reconciliation

Toxic parents will expect and demand that you let go of the past and not hold them accountable for their behavior. Rather than feeling remorse and looking to earn trust back, they feel they are entitled to it and are offended or angered when you expect that they change or cease their disrespect, harmful behavior, or abuse before relationship can happen.

17: Hypocrisy

Toxic parents will treat others with overt disrespect but will get incredibly offended when they detect the same type of treatment from others in the slightest. For example, they will demand and expect from others without a thought of how they feel, what they need and how it affects them to give as much as they are, but if someone tells the narcissist no they will accuse that person of being selfish.

18: Jealousy of others

Toxic parents will be jealous of others success and skill and will try one-up someone who has demonstrated success or skill to get the attention onto them, or they might try to down-play another's ability or achievements. For example, if you say you scored 195 the last time you went bowling, they will "that's not that great, that's easy" or "I once got 200 when I went bowling."

19: Overly concerned with image to others

Toxic parents want to appear perfect, successful, and glamorous to others. They will work very hard trying to put up a good image and impress others by acting a certain way around others and buying the biggest and best of different things. They love showing off what they think makes them better than others, whether it is possessions, accomplishments, or their successful children. They go out of their way to seek <u>attention</u> and flattery to boost their egos. They might go into excessive debt to keep the most up to date model of car or speedboat, or to remodel the house or buy a new house when the house, boat, or car they have is perfectly fine.

20: Inability to admit to wrong

When confronted by someone they have hurt, toxic parents will normally gaslight. If gaslighting doesn't work, they will become defensive and make excuses or shift the blame to the adult child and attack them. Their egos are so fragile it is very rare that a narcissist can admit fault, unless they are doing so to manipulate.

21: Trouble maintaining relationships

Although relationships can be tricky and we've all experienced broken relationships at some time in our lives, toxic parents will have a history of severely damaged relationships. Lack of friendships are also very common with toxic parents.

Although these are the most common behaviors you will see with toxic parents, this does not cover all of them. If none of these behaviors describe what a toxic parent or in-laws is doing or saying to you, but being around them makes you feel devalued, stressed, anxious, guilt ridden or controlled, it's likely a toxic behavior.

SECTION 2
BOUNDARIES

CHAPTER 2:
BOUNDARIES – THE KEY TO
DEALING WITH TOXIC PARENTS

What Boundaries Are.

I often see confusion around the meaning of boundaries. Selfish parents will often label boundaries as selfish, controlling or punishing and if we do not understand what boundaries are, we can fall for these lies and allow ourselves to be swayed from setting needed boundaries. So let's be clear on the actual meaning of what boundaries are: **Boundaries are limits on what we allow people to do to us, or on what we will do to others.** It is all about controlling what we allow in and out of our lives. Boundaries are not about changing other's behavior, that is a demand and is crossing other's boundaries, instead we are limiting our exposure to certain things and not allowing certain things to be done to us. Here are some examples of demand and boundaries:

Demands: "You'd better stop that." "I expect you to ____ in the future."

Boundaries: "I would like this to stop." "I am not comfortable with being talked to that way."

As you can see, demands are about getting someone to do something or stop something, whereas boundaries let others know what we are comfortable with or will not tolerate.

Why Set Boundaries.

Setting boundaries with others can be scary. Toxic parents can get upset at us, and yell at us, and we can deal with a lot of guilt. Here are some important reasons for setting boundaries we should keep in mind to help motivate us to stay strong:

1: We enhance our relationships with others.

Just because people are frequently in the same proximity, it doesn't mean they have a healthy relationship, or even a real relationship for that matter. Behaviors such as control, manipulation, negativity, passive-aggression, criticism, and entitlement are poisonous to a relationship. These behaviors are like weeds in a garden that choke the life out of the plants of love, respect and trust. If we realize this we can see that setting boundaries is not about rejection or being mean, it is an invitation to someone else for a healthy relationship. You are offering someone an opportunity to enter into a more loving and respectful connection with you. If setting boundaries with toxic behavior causes that relationship to end, then your relationship with that person wasn't really a relationship to begin with.

2: We preserve our ability to love and forgive.

It is much harder to love someone when the behavior is continually happening to us; setting limits to where the person can no longer do that thing makes it much easier to love (be loving?). When we love and care for ourselves by protecting ourselves from disrespect and valuing our emotions and mental health, we protect our ability to love and care for others. The same with forgiveness. It's much easier to forgive someone after one or a few offenses that are no longer happening rather than staying in a situation where an offense is continually repeating. Setting boundaries protects your heart from further hurt and mistreatment and preserves your ability to love and extend grace to others. Without boundaries you are more likely to become resentful and bitter. Don't believe me? Talk to woman who left a bad marriage after 30 years of abuse, versus a woman who left a boyfriend after the first time he hit her. Who do you think is less likely to be bitter and carry unforgiveness?

3: We have more time and energy for the things we should give time and energy too.

Selfish and greedy parents aren't concerned with you having enough time for your spouse

and kids, to recharge yourself, or to do things you want to do, they care mostly or all about

themselves. And there are lots of selfish and greedy people in the world I'm afraid, whether friends, family, or work relationships. Without boundaries, selfish and greedy people will suck up too much of your time and energy and then you won't have enough for the things you should prioritize such as your spouse, kids and/or other relationships, or self-growth and development.

4: Our emotional and mental health is at risk when we don't set boundaries.

Although we cannot completely eliminate negative behavior towards us, in fact some

negative behavior is good because it builds our resiliency, too much is not good for us. Especially in our closer relationships such as parents. Frequent devaluing, disrespectful or controlling behavior will inevitably diminish our self-worth, self-esteem, and sense of autonomy. Depression, anxiety, addictions and other mental health problems are sure to follow when we have little to no boundaries.

5: Not setting boundaries is an act of unkindness.

Many feel setting boundaries is being mean, but did you know that when we don't set boundaries, that is when we are actually the most mean and unloving?

Here's why:

- **Not setting boundaries hurts other people.** When we don't set boundaries, we are enabling the parent to continue their behavior not only to us, but to other people. We are helping them hurt others.

- **Not setting boundaries hurts the toxic person.** A selfish and disrespectful person is an unhappy person, while a kind and respectful person is a happy person. When we don't set boundaries and allow disrespect or mistreatment, we are rescuing the person from necessary feedback the natural consequences of their negative behaviors, which is necessary for them to grow. Because of this, they are more likely to stay stuck in this cycle of mistreating others, and they stay miserable throughout their life.

- **Not setting boundaries is being uncaring towards ourselves, which is just as wrong as being uncaring towards another person.** There's a universal standard that we are to be kind to others that are in our proximity, and more importantly stand up for those that are wronged. We forget that the reason for this is that others are human beings, sacred created life worthy of respect and care. WE are that too! You and I are human beings, worthy of respect and care. We have a duty to protect and care for ourselves just as much as anyone else, because we are human beings too! It's just as wrong to not stand up for ourselves when we are being mistreated, as it is to allow someone else to be mistreated and do nothing.

WHAT BEHAVIORS TO SET BOUNDARIES WITH

You may be asking yourself how do I know when to set boundaries? Here is a list of 9 of the most common behaviors you will experience with toxic parents that I recommend you set boundaries with.

1: Control.

Telling you what to do, or demanding you do or give them something rather than asking you.

2: Manipulation.

Try to make you feel a certain way (usually a negative feeling) to get you to do what they want. Most common way is to act wounded, sad or lonely to get you to feel guilty.

3: Criticism.

Speaking negatively about you or your choices. They are entitled to their own thoughts and opinions but saying negative things to you shouldn't be allowed.

4: Acting entitled.

Acting as though what belongs to you belongs to them, and taking, touching, using without asking or without permission.

5: Being argumentative about different view or opinions.

Trying to force you to agree with their viewpoints.

6: Disrespecting noes.

Acting angry, hostile, pushing back, or guilt tripping when you say no.

7: Crossing boundaries.

Reacting poorly when you set a boundary, refusing to agree to respect a boundary or continuing a behavior towards you or your parents when you have communicated the behavior is unwanted.

8: Insults.

Saying negative or devaluing things about you or your choices.

9: Lecturing/unsolicited advice.

Telling you what you should or shouldn't be doing when you did not ask for their opinion and they did not ask if they could share it.

Do not limit your boundaries to just these behaviors. If there is anything else that bothers you or your spouse, it is your right and duty to speak up and vocalize what is hurting you. But if you set boundaries with your parents (or in-laws) with at least these 9 behaviors, your relationships with significantly improve and the stress in your life or marriage will greatly be reduced.

CHAPTER 3:
SETTING BOUNDARIES WITH YOUR PARTNER OR SPOUSE'S PARENTS

So you're married or in a serious relationship and come to find out one or more of your partner's parents are toxic. What do you do? I believe it is ok to set boundaries with smaller issues with in-laws or soon-to-be in-laws, but when they are toxic and the issues are bigger, I believe it is best for each person to set boundaries with their own families of origin for a few reasons:

Offense is much more likely to occur when the non-relative partner brings up an issue rather than the relative. Sometimes this is not the case because the non-relative partner is more tactful, but in most cases I see the parents are more easily offended when a non-relative partner addresses them.

It is much harder for the non-relative partner to confront their in-laws about issues. There is a natural desire to be liked by one's in-laws and it can be more devastating to not be. Having to have tough conversations with in-laws, especially in the earlier years of marriage, can be very stressful for the non-relative partner. It is generally much easier for the relative partner to confront his or her own parents.

So if you are having issues with an in-laws or in-laws being toxic, I highly suggest you ask your partner to be the one to set the boundaries with his or her own parents. However, the way you go about this makes all the difference. Our own families of origin can be a sensitive topic for us all and it should be addressed with tact and sensitivity. Follow these steps to improve your chances of gaining your spouse's cooperation.

Avoid...

1. Criticizing their parents or their parent's behavior.
2. Getting angry and criticizing your spouse.
3. Pushing or pressuring your spouse to set boundaries with his or her parents.

Do...

1. Share how you FEEL when your partner's parents do or say the things they do. <u>There is power when your spouse knows how you feel!</u>
   - "I feel disrespected when your mother critiques how I decorate

the house and tells me how to decorate without me asking."
- "I feel disrespected when your parents show up to the house unannounced."

2. Share what you NEED.
    - I would like it if you asked your mother to ask before giving me advice or waited until I asked her for advice.
    - I need you to tell your parents to ask before coming over.

If Your Spouse Will Not Cooperate.

If your spouse wants to set boundaries but they are having a really hard time, or if they will not work with you, value your feelings and needs and make adjustments, there is a few different actions you can take.

1. Get counseling together. This is beneficial for two reasons.
    - It is hard for someone who has not realized how toxic his or her parents are to take their partner's word for it all of the sudden. Having a person on the outside speak into the situation that is a professional nonetheless can help your partner see their parent's

toxicity. When looking for a counselor, ask them if they have experience dealing with toxic or narcissistic parents before booking. You do not want to find a counselor who is an enabler and takes the toxic parent's side.

- When a partner does not want to work with you when you share how their parent's behavior bothers you, this shows a lack of value for your feelings. A counselor can spot this and challenge your partner to consider your feelings over their parent's and whether they believe your feelings are rational or not.

2. Set boundaries with his or her parents yourself. If a partner or spouse refuses to set boundaries with their parent, even after getting counseling (or if they refuse to do this), know you cannot control your partner, but you can communicate boundaries with their parents and limit your exposure to their toxic behavior yourself if they continue the behavior. Some examples of how to do this is...

- Saying you're not ok with them coming over.

- Staying in your room or leave house when they come over.

Be cautious to not do this to punish your partner or spouse or get back at them. Do it to protect yourself from your in-law's poor behavior. I would even encourage you to have a conversation with your spouse where you let them know you aren't doing these things to punish them, but to protect yourself from their parents' behavior because it's effecting you very poorly.

CHAPTER 4:
HOW TO SET BOUNDARIES

3 Steps to Set Boundaries Gently.

When setting boundaries with a parent for the first time, I suggest a more diplomatic approach. If the behavior continues (which we'll talk about in the next chapter), then move to a firmer approach. Here are three steps for setting boundaries the first time, which I call *gentle boundaries*.

1: Prepare the person for a conversation.

You want to let the person know you are not trying to attack them by what you are going to say, and you are sharing this because you want a better relationship with them. Let them know you value them and your relationship. Remember the song from Mary Poppins "I spoonful of sugar helps the medicine go down"? This is very much true, unless they are toxic, which we will deal with in the next chapter. But for most cases, saying some kind words first will help them be less likely to feel hurt or attacked by what you say, and listen to where you're coming from.

2: Share how you feel and don't judge their behavior.

Many people tend to focus on what the other person did and proclaim this as bad behavior in order to get what they are needing or get the person to change. For example:

- What you did was selfish/mean/rude/disrespectful.
- You are so selfish/rude/mean.
- Why do you ALWAYS do that?
- Why can't you ever just...
- You just have to...don't you?

Unfortunately this works horribly! When we speak negatively about someone else or their behavior, they feel attacked. And what do people do when they feel attacked? They defend, attack back, or retreat! For example, a person who feels verbally attacked will make excuses for why they did what they did (defend), they might start pointing out what you do or say wrong or put the blame on you (attack back), or they might shut down and not engage in a conversation or go to another room (retreat). When this happens the person who had the issue feels unheard or attacked or both and starts attacking more aggressively. I'm sure you can guess what will continue to happen.

This can often be avoided if we *focus on what we are feeling and needing rather than the other person or their behavior*. Try communicating using one of the following phrases.

- I felt hurt when you said _____.
- I feel disrespected when you _____.

3: Ask them for what you need changed.

Try using the phrase "it would mean a lot to me if you could stop" or "I would really appreciate it if you could not" then share what you are wanting them to stop. Using those phrases are very vulnerable and helps keep the conversation on your feelings and needs rather than on the person's behavior. This will help them be thinking about how you feel rather than wanting to defend themself.

What To Do When You Get A Negative Response.

Sometimes no matter how nice you are you will get a negative reaction from someone such

as anger or sulking. Here's what to do for each scenario:

Sulking/pouting/crying

If they sulk or pout, sometimes they are feeling rejected or unliked, but often it is manipulation to get you to change your boundary mixed with a little rejection. You can reaffirm your love and care for them and reassure them and ask them if there is something you can do or say to help them feel better, but if after doing this they are still acting victimized, it is safe to know they are just wanting what they want and are trying to manipulate rather than looking for love. Be kind but put don't get into an argument or debate where you are explaining yourself or justifying your boundary or no (more on this later). Shut down the conversation if they keep trying to argue or manipulate after you have shown empathy and tried to comfort them.

Anger

If they get angry, you can reaffirm them of your love and care as well, but just once. Often anger is a sign of selfishness. They believe that they have a right to treat you how they want or get what they want from you. There is no need to feel guilty or bad if they are mad, they are the selfish ones. Hold strong! You can empathize if someone gets angry and offer to do or say something that will help them feel better, but do not stay around or on the phone if they yell, get hostile or insulting. If they start to do this, tell them you're happy to hear what they have to say as long as they can stay calm and respectful. If they continue yelling or insulting, leave or hang up the phone.

SETTING BOUNDARIES FIRMLY

Firm boundaries are for parents you know don't respond well to boundaries, or if what your parents have done is something very hurtful or disrespectful. When it is quite clear they are toxic and are not going to take boundaries well that is when you need to get firmer. No more diplomacy, you need to lay down the law. Here are two steps to dealing with the parent or in-law who won't respect your boundaries.

2 Steps to Set Boundaries Firmly

1: Tell them the behavior you'd like them to stop.

When you do this, do not pose it as a question. When it's your first time setting a boundary you give them the benefit of a doubt and assume your parent/in-law could be respectful. But if in previous times you have set a boundary, they are disrespectful or unsafe, they have lost that privilege. Now if you present your boundary as a question, these types of parents will take it as optional and will not comply or take it as an invitation to push back. However, you also want to make sure you do not present the boundary as a demand. When we demand from others or tell them what to do or not do, not only are we attempting to control them and are being toxic ourselves, but this will most assuredly cause an uncooperative response from them. Instead say the boundary as a communication of what you want or need. Try using one of the following phrases:

"I need this stop..."

"I would like this to stop..."

"I do not appreciate that..."

"I do not like it when you do that..."

2: Ask if they can agree to stop the behavior.

You want to get verbal confirmation from them that they will agree to stop the unwanted behavior. This way you are making it clear exactly what you need, and their response will be clear on if they are going to agree to your boundary or not. If you just say "I don't like that, and need it to stop," a toxic parent is likely to just get upset, offended, gaslight or try to argue, and it is unclear what they are deciding. If you ask if they can agree to stop the behavior, if the next words out of their mouth are not "yes," (can be in different words) it is clear they are saying no.

In the next chapter we will talk about what to do if they do not agree.

CHAPTER 5:
WHAT TO DO WHEN TOXIC PARENTS DON'T RESPECT YOUR BOUNDARIES

Toxic parents will most often not agree to respect your boundary straight away. Instead what they will often do is...

- act very wounded
- get angry and try to intimidate you
- argue with your boundary
- refuse to respect your boundary
- twist what you are saying
- gaslight you (tell you you're overreacting, being overly sensitive, they were just joking, or they don't remember it happening)

Most of these things are to get you caught up in an argument to change your mind about the boundary, or to punish you for setting a boundary.

The key to dealing with this, is to not engage in an argument. Do not try to argue with them. Do not try to fight with them or convince them you're right. Do not explain yourself or justify why you're setting a boundary. If you do this, THEY HAVE WON!

Instead, if a toxic parent tries to push back, argue, gaslight, or guilt trip, do the following three things:

1: Ignore what they said and tell them what you will be doing if they continue the behavior continues.

Have an action planned that will protect you from the person's negative behavior if they continue to do it. These actions are called *consequences*. Let them know what the consequence will be if the behavior continues (more in this soon). Boundary consequences are not punishments towards the person crossing our boundaries, they are things we do to protect ourselves from their behavior. Do not sound threatening when you do this, and do not pose it as a way to sound controlling. You are simply letting the person know what you will be doing if the behavior continues.

Some examples of how to say this are:

- If this continues I will be leaving or hanging up the phone
- If you cannot agree to stop this behavior, I will not be spending time with you until you can

Possible consequences you can use are...

- Leaving
- Hanging up a phone
- Seeing or talking with the person less
- Not allowing them to spend time with your kids without you present
- Not giving something or doing someone for someone
- Not talking to or seeing the person at all

2: Don't get caught up in an argument.

Selfish and toxic parents who don't respect boundaries have a magical way of getting you

caught up in an argument when you set a boundary or say no. They try to argue to either get you to change your mind, and if you do not they throw everything they can at you to punish you by making you feel guilty, shamed, or worthless. It is really quite diabolical. You can avoid all of this by not letting an argument happen.

You can do this by showing care and empathy for how they feel if they are hurt or upset, but also say you have made your decision and you do not want to argue about it. If they keep trying to argue do not engage with them, just tell them that if they cannot drop the subject you will leave or hang up the phone and do just that if they continue. This might seem mean, but trust me when I say, a toxic person's intention in arguing about your boundary is to either control you or punish you. You don't deserve to be treated that way. Take care of yourself by not letting them suck you in.

3: Follow through with the consequence if the behavior still continues or they refuse to agree to respect your boundary.

When parents choose not to respect respecting your boundaries and continue with the behavior or flat out refuse when you present the boundary, follow through with the consequence (the action to protect yourself from their behavior).   You basically remove or limit the object or person that is at the receiving end of the bad behavior. If the behavior is towards you, you remove yourself from the situation, and limit time with them if it continues. If the behavior is with your kids you stop letting them babysit or spend time with them alone. Although consequences bring up to mind the thought of punishing, I am not speaking of punishment at all. Consequences are simply the result or effect of an action. What we are doing when we remove ourselves from a toxic situation is allowing someone to experience the negative result of their behavior. As I mentioned earlier, we are not trying to change the parent, this is controlling and again, it is not done to hurt or punish the parent. **This action should be done *only* to protect yourself from or limit the toxic behavior of the perpetrator.**

DEALING WITH GASLIGHTING

Gaslighting is when you try to bring up an issue with a someone or set a boundary, and they invalidate your perception of their behavior or what happened. This is something you will commonly experience with toxic parents. Toxic parents can try to gaslight you in several different ways:

- They might say you're being overly sensitive.
- They might say you're remembering things wrong
- They might say they didn't mean the behavior or something they said the way you're interpreting it. (This is the most common).
- They might play dumb and say they don't remember saying or doing that.

How to Know If You Are Right or Not

How can we tell if we are being overly sensitive or remembering things wrong, or if our perception is valid? One way to know this is by asking yourself how long you've known the person. If it's your parent, chances are you know them pretty well and can tell when they are being dishonest or what they mean when they do or say certain things. Also ask yourself if this person has a history of being dishonest with you? And lastly, ask for input from a friend. Tell them your experience, what was said and done, and get outside input to see if you are being overly or appropriately sensitive.

How to Deal with Gaslighting

Regardless of how someone meant actions or words towards you, you have a right to set a boundary if it bothers you. So when you set a boundary, and someone says you're being oversensitive, unfair, they didn't mean it the way you think they did, or that you're remembering it wrong, here's what to do:

- Ignore the gaslighting. You read that right, don't get into an argument or debate with them about who is wrong and who is right, it will get you nowhere but frustrated. Just dismiss the gaslighting and...
- Reiterate the boundary. Examples:
  o "Regardless, I would like this behavior to stop, can I count on you to stop (unwanted behavior)?"
  o "I understand we have a difference of opinion, but I would still like this

behavior to stop, can I count on you to stop (unwanted behavior)?"

o "We seem to be remembering things differently, that's ok. Can you still agree to not do (unwanted behavior).

If they keep trying to gaslight when you say this, or begin to argue, yell, or manipulate, tell them the boundary is not up debate and tell them what you will be doing if the behavior continues (consequence). If they keep trying to argue, gaslight or manipulate, you leave or hang up the phone and implement the consequence.

So altogether that would sound like...

You: Mom/Dad I feel disrespected when you say do ____, would you mind not doing that?

Gaslighter: "I think you're being oversensitive" or "I didn't mean it like that."

You: I understand, but I would like that behavior to stop still, can I count on you to do that?

Gaslighter: Why are you being like this? Can't I say anything without you getting so defensive?

You: Mom/Dad, I love you but this is not up for debate, if this happens again I will leave/hang up. Can you agree to stop?

Gaslighter: What is your problem? Why are you being like this? Can't I say anything?

You:* Leave/hang up the phone

In the next section we will discuss going no contact with toxic parents and dealing with the aftermath and repercussions.

SECTION 3
GOING NO CONTACT AND DEALING WITH THE AFTERMATH

CHAPTER 6:
THE ART OF NO CONTACT

Going no contact simply means to stop being in contact with someone. This can be something you do permanently until your toxic parent changes their behavior or temporarily while you are healing from trauma. You stop seeing them and talking with them. I do not suggest going no contact quickly, not because you owe your parents to be in relationship with them but because cutting parents off too easily can cause numerous problems for *you*. Here are some examples:

- **Cutting off parents without trying to set and enforce boundaries first easily becomes a habit where we run from difficult situations**. Because all people are imperfect (including you and I), we will quickly find ourselves very alone and isolated when our solution to tough problems in relationships is to cut someone off rather than setting and enforcing boundaries.
- **When we cut off people permanently because of our triggers rather than their**

toxicity, we deceive ourselves into thinking that this solves the problem when the real problem is our unresolved trauma. If being around a person is triggering (especially if they were the reason for our trauma), it is healthy to take space from them, but we should also work on healing our emotional trauma until we can gain the courage to face these people and set and enforce boundaries.

- **Running from a difficult situation (which we can be doing when we cut people off too quickly) rather than facing it creates cowardice within us**. We allow fear to win and become stronger within us. While facing our fears creates courage and boosts your self-confidence.

WHEN YOU SHOULD GO NO CONTACT

This is why I suggest you do what you can to set and *enforce* boundaries first without not putting your mental health in jeopardy.

Good reasons you should go no contact with a parent:

- Your parent's behavior is causing you, your kids or your marriage stress, or poorly affecting your mental health by making you feel controlled, or devalued to the point the relationship is more bad than good for you to be in.

AND...

You have communicated with your parents or in-laws, tried setting boundaries but they refuse to stop the behavior, they say they will stop behavior but don't, or whenever you bring up the issues they gaslight, argue, attack, etc.

- Your mental health is suffering and you're needing to heal but their presence and contact with them is triggering you and keeping you stuck with your trauma. (When this is the case I suggest you work on your trauma until you can get to a place where you can try setting boundaries with them.

- They have done something so terrible, hurtful or abusive, you cannot trust them again. There is no apology to fix it, what they did was just so horrible, that you can safely say they are not a good person to be in relationship with, and they are far from being a good relationship for you. And maybe this might be for a time, or it could permanent it's up to you and what you think is best for you and your family.

HOW TO GO NO CONTACT

To let them know or not let them know, that is the question. For most scenarios I suggest informing the toxic parent that you are not wanting contact. If you do not, they are certainly going to still try to contact you, or show up to your house, or what have you. Don't get me wrong, toxic parents or other parents will often still do this even after being informed you do not want contact, but at least this way they are clearly the ones that are being rude if they still try to contact you. This will help you with not feeling guilty.

The times you should not let them know, is if they are very emotionally abusive and you have a lot of emotional trauma. In this instance where you will probably be the subject of a tongue lashing, it might be better for you to just stop contacting them or responding to their attempts to contact you.

But for those that can say something, here are three options and example conversations for letting your toxic parent know your will no longer be in contact.

1. **Letting them know with a chance for them to fix the relationship (recommended).**
   "Mum/Dad/Greg/Rachel, since you cannot agree to stop the behaviors I have asked you

to stop, I will no longer be talking with or seeing you until you do. Please do not reach out to me unless you are informing me that you agree to make the changes I need for our relationship to move forward. If you continue to contact me without agreeing to make the needed changes, I will be blocking you on all forms of contact.

2. **Letting them know you want permanent no contact.**
    "Mom/Dad, I have found out relationship to be hurtful/disrespectful/abusive and I will not be in contact with you and do not want to be contacted. If you continue to try to contact me other than for emergencies (optional) you will be blocked on all form of communication.

3. **Letting them know you are taking space temporarily.** "Mom/Dad, I am dealing with a lot at the moment, and our relationship has been tough at this time. I will be taking some space while I work on myself, and I am asking that you respect that and not try to reach out to me until I am ready for contact."

In the next chapter we will discuss missing the toxic parent or doubting your decision after going no contact.

CHAPTER 7:
MISSING THE TOXIC PARENT AND DOUBTING YOUR DECISION

Our brains do this lovely thing when we lose a relationship, whether from death, distance, break up or going no contact with someone. It likes to remember all of the good things and forget the bad, and then we miss the person. This can be nice as we remember a wonderful person that we have lost through death, but it makes going no contact with a narcissistic or toxic parent difficult. We forget about all of the disrespect and emotional abuse and begin to wonder if we made the right choice. Our memory distorts and we begin to think maybe we were too hasty, or perhaps we were in the wrong. Here is how to deal with this.

Get a notepad and write down all of the problems you were having with toxic parent.

The control, the manipulation, the belittling, the blow ups or guilt trips when you'd say no, the disrespect, the demands and entitlement. Write down all of it. Everything you can remember. *Be sure to write down specific examples of what they did.* For example instead of writing:

"They were manipulative/controlling/disrespectful/emotionally abusive, etc."

You will want to write something like...

"They were manipulative, *such as when she/he would make me feel bad when I would say no or couldn't come see them every day."*

"They didn't have any empathy. *She/he would blow up at me whenever I would share how she/he hurt me and didn't care about how her behavior affected me."*

Read over the list whenever you start to miss them or second guess yourself.

Reading these things to yourself will remind you of why you cut them off which will help you miss them less (though not entirely) and stop doubting your decision.

CHAPTER 8:
DEALING WITH ENABLERS

What an Enabler Is

Enablers are people (usually other family members) that perpetuate, support and excuse bad behavior in our parents. They refuse to hold the toxic parent accountable, instead they take their side and/or bully and pressure the victim of the toxic person's abuse or mistreatment to break no contact and not have boundaries.

Some common things enablers do are:

- Make excuses for the things toxic parents in your life have done instead of asking questions about what you experienced and how you feel.
- Throw all of these suggestions at you for how you should fix the relationship with the toxic person, rather than worrying about what is best for you and your family.
- Show more value and care for the toxic person getting what they want than your mental health and whether you are treated well or not.

- They will actually gaslight you, they will say things like, "are you sure you're not being overly sensitive?" "they didn't mean it like that," "they wouldn't say that," "it's just their personality," and "they don't mean anything by it."

What to Do About Them

The biggest key to dealing with enablers is to **not argue with them!** If you've explained what happened and how you feel to someone, and they just make excuses or invalidate your perception, it's because they have codependency issues which means they have put the toxic person on a pedestal and they can do no wrong. They're self-worth is tied up in keeping this person happy whether it is a friend or parent (often this is the case with children and parents). They feel extremely responsible for this person's feelings, and they will disrespect and even emotionally abuse others to keep this person happy. Nothing you say will change the enabler's mind. Trying to convince them of your viewpoint will just frustrate you and give them more of a chance to make you feel bad for protecting yourself and your family.

How to not get into an argument with an enabler.

When an enabler tries to push you to talk with a

toxic parent you have set boundary with or cut off, or if they are making excuses for their behavior, here are steps you can take to shut the conversation down.

1. **Tell them you are not looking for advice on the subject.**
   - E.g. "Thank you for trying to help, but I'm not looking for advice on this at the moment.

2. **If they keep pushing ask them not to push you to not have boundaries with the toxic parent.**
   - E.g. "Again, thank you for trying to help, but I have made my decision, would you mind not trying to convince me to talk to (parent's name)?

3. **If they try to argue with this, shut the conversation down.**
   You can do this by...
   - Telling them you're not wanting to talk about that topic and asking again if they can stop pushing you.
   - If they keep trying to argue after you tell them this, warn them that you would like the conversation to stop, and if they keep going you will hang up the phone or leave the situation.

○ Example:

Enabler: (still pushing you after the last two steps)

You: Hey I've asked to stop trying to convince me to talk (parent's name) and I am not feeling like what I am asking is being respected, if we can't drop the subject I am going to need to leave/hang up the phone.

Moving forward, if they don't ever do this again, you can have relationship with them if you want, but if they continue to bring the situation up and try to manipulate or pressure you to change your mind I would suggest you stop talking to them as well as the toxic parent. Essentially this person is toxic as well.

CHAPTER 9:
SMEAR CAMPAIGNS

Smear campaigns are when a toxic person defames you and slanders you to everyone else in the parents or circle of friends after you go no contact, and even to a more public audience such as on social media. Some examples are they might say you're mean, you're crazy, you're controlling, you cut them off for no reason, or some other story without sharing the real reason why you cut them off.

How do you handle this?

The best thing you can do is ignore it! The good people in your life will see through the garbage or at the very least they will ask you for your side of the story. Healthy people that are somewhat involved in your life and know your parents or in-laws will be able to see through the lies and see there is more to it than what the toxic parent is saying.

For the people that believe what the toxic parent says and simply takes their word for it, get on your knees and thank God. You have just found out what their true colors are!

People will generally only take a toxic person's side if that person is toxic themselves, and you don't want those people in your life. Your life has just been made easier. Let them go and stop talking to these people as well as the toxic parent.

CHAPTER 10:
WHAT TO DO IF THEY BREAK NO CONTACT

What do we do when toxic parents we have cut off keep trying to contact us or see us? Here are some answers that I have seen work best for myself and others.

When they try contact you via phone call, text, or social media.

The best thing to do is to block them on all forms of digital communication. Cell phone, Facebook, email, Instagram, Twitter, Tik-Tok. Block them on everything. If they try to call or text from a different email address of phone number, change your phone number or email address. If you have given them the option that they can make amends if they so choose, leave a digital communication option open (I recommend email) and let them know if they choose to agree to your boundaries that is how they can contact you.

If they show up to your door.

Do not answer the door. You are not obligated to answer the door for them. You are not being rude THEY are. If they stay at the door and do not leave, you might consider called the police. You could even check with your city or county to see if a restraining order is possible. If need be, I would consider moving. I know moving is a major step, but sometimes that is best for your peace of mind, so you aren't worrying about them show up to your door.

If they send letters or packages for you or your kids.

There is kind of a grey area on what to do here. One thing I recommend you not do is write the toxic parent you've gone no contact with back. Do not engage. But there is division on agreement by most relationship experts on whether someone should ignore the letters and packages or reject the mail or packages. Here is a case for both:

- If you do not send packages/presents for kids back but ignore them or donate them, you are not breaking no contact, but the toxic parent can assume you are keeping them and using them, and feel they have an in with you to manipulate their way back in your life.
- If you write return to sender back on the box, you are breaking the no contact rule in a sense, but the message you are sending

them is "you can't manipulate me, so you might as well give up."

I have tried both ways, and what worked for my wife and I with people we've gone no contact with is the sending the packages or letters back unopened. But you try writing return to sender on letters or packages first for a few times, and if it doesn't work simply throw them out or donate them.

CHAPTER 11:
EXPLAINING TO YOUR KIDS WHY THEY CAN'T SEE THEIR GRANDPARENTS

I get asked a lot by parents that have gone no contact with a very toxic parent how they can explain it to their children.

In my opinion the best approach to do this is to be honest. Do not make attacks about your toxic parent or parent's character, and do not be excessively negative, but do be truthful and up front with your child at an appropriate age about the toxic parent's behavior.

The way to do this is by focusing on your parent's (or parent's) behavior rather than making statements about their character. For example...

Instead of saying:

"grandma/grandpa is a jerk, horrible person, nasty, toxic, etc.,"

You say:

"grandma/grandpa was *being* very unkind, hurtful,

or toxic, we tried talking to him/her multiple times, but he/she chose to not change their hurtful behavior. So we do not spend time with her."

This can also be a great teaching moment where you explain to your child that you don't spend a lot of time with people that chose to treat you poorly even when you communicate with them. Your children will learn healthy boundaries by your example.

CHAPTER 12:
WHEN YOU HAVE TO STILL SEE THEM

For some people going no contact with the narcissist is not an option. Some of the situations where this is the case might be when:

- You are coparenting with a narcissist, taking care of someone who is ill or dying
- You are wanting to attend a funeral or a wedding
- You are not wanting to break contact with someone because it would mean not being able to see someone else
- You are not able to leave a parent because of financial dependency for the present time, or maybe you are not emotionally ready.
- If you find that you cannot leave because of a financial situation or because it is emotionally difficult for you (if this is your situation I would encourage you to work towards a place where you are able to be financially dependent or emotionally strong enough to take that step).

For those of you who cannot avoid a narcissist because of other reasons or if you really do not want to break contact, there is something else you can do to largely minimize the effects of their emotional abuse: *grey-rocking.* Grey-rocking is when you **act indifferent** to the attempts of the narcissist to guilt trip you, gaslight you, belittle you, criticize you, or shame you. You act as if you do not care; cold and aloof. In this way you are like a "grey rock." By acting like you do not care, it helps you actually not care about the narcissist's toxic behavior and attempts to get to you. It makes you more unphased by their attempts to get a rise out of you. The narcissist gets frustrated by this (which is enjoyable for you) but it often leads them to give up trying, because they are not getting what they are so desperately looking for when they try to trigger you, *attention!*

Although grey rocking is quite effective, I do not suggest that this be your go action plan if you find someone in your life is a narcissist. It does not completely protect you from the negative effects of disrespectful and emotionally abusive treatment, and your life is too short to have people around you that you do not mutually share love and respect with.

There are two things I suggest you do to learn how to grey-rock, and I suggest you practice these by yourself before using them with a narcissist. The *first* thing I suggest you practice is having a blank, bored expression on your face. You want to relax your face muscles, neither smiling nor frowning. Relax your eyelids or let them droop. The *second* thing you want to practice is short 1-2-word responses. Memorize the following words and phrases if it helps:

"Yep"

"Nope"

"Maybe"

"Probably"

"Guess so"

"Guess not"

"Could be"

"Don't know"

Here is an example of how to use these terms.

Narcissist: "So you're not going to be at _____, and you're just doing your own thing?"

You: "Yup."

Narcissist: "How can you do that? You are so selfish!

You: "Guess so."

Narcissist: "I'm trying to have a conversation with you! Can't you say anything more than one-word answers?"

You: "Nah."

Narcissist: "I guess you don't even care then."

You: "Guess not."

Narcissist: "Something is seriously wrong with you."

You: "Probably."

Practice this before dealing with a narcissist. Look in a mirror and practice your bored, indifferent face, and imagine the narcissist saying things they normally do, and practice giving the very short 1-2-word responses.

WARNING: Be sure to not use this method in a situation where the narcissist can get violent. At first the narcissist can get frustrated and angry that they cannot get the attention and control they are seeking. It can be rather enjoyable to watch, if it does not turn dangerous for you. Make sure you are not at risk of physical harm before attempting grey-rocking.

CHAPTER 13:
DEALING WITH GUILT

Many people who set boundaries (or go no contact) with parents deal with tremendous guilt. **The source of this guilt comes from false beliefs and distorted thought patterns we carry about ourselves and others.** We must become aware of what these lies are and challenge them if we want to learn to set boundaries without guilt and move past fear of what others think or their emotions.

The biggest problem I see my clients make when they deal with guilt over setting boundaries, is they often try to tell themselves that they are NOT doing anything wrong or that they are NOT responsible for anyone's feelings. Unfortunately our subconscious mind doesn't hear the word NOT, it will only expound and magnify what we focus on. Realizing we are not responsible or not doing anything wrong is helpful, but if we are telling ourselves that we are not doing something wrong, or not responsible for other's feelings, we are focusing on doing something wrong and being responsible for other's feelings, and the subconscious will magnify this feeling. How do we fix this? A negative feeling (such as guilt) is a lot like darkness. Darkness cannot be pushed out, light (it's opposite) needs to come in and replace the darkness. To remove guilt, we need to replace it with the opposite feeling. The opposite of feeling guilty or bad, is feeling proud or good about yourself.

Here is a list of the most common lies people believe that cause guilt and truths to counter the lies and create a sense of pride and healthy self-esteem:

Lie 1: Saying no is selfish or mean.

Truth: It is good for you to manage how much you give to and do for others, and to protect yourself from disrespectful or devaluing situations. It actually helps you love others and give to others more in the long run. When you always say yes and allow others to use you too much and take advantage of you, it diminishes your ability to give to and do for others out of love.

Lie 2: Boundaries are mean.

Truth: Setting boundaries is not mean, it is being kind to and protecting yourself. And being kind to and protecting yourself, is just as good a noble as protecting someone else, because you're a human being too. When you protect yourself from disrespectful behavior or abuse, you also protect your ability to genuinely love others.

Lie 3: If someone is hurt when I set a boundary, it is because I did something wrong.

Truth: When someone is hurt when you set a boundary, you are not hurting them, **they are hurting themselves.** Boundaries are not offensive in nature, they are defensive. Boundaries are about protection not attacking or purposefully hurting someone. When someone is hurt by another person protecting themself, it is because that person was attacking the other person; *they were in the wrong not the person protecting themself!*

Lie 4: If someone is hurt when I say no it is because I did something wrong.

Truth: When parents are hurt when you say no, it is because of their own expectations or perceptions, not because you hurt them or did something wrong to them. It is good to give and do for others, but it is also good to say no when you feel you have given or done enough, and to situations where you feel disrespected, used or controlled. Saying no in these situations is not being bad or selfish, it is being kind and good to yourself! Which is just as important as being kind and good to others.

Lie 5: I am obligated to keep others happy.

Truth: You are obligated to be kind to others as long as long as it doesn't get in the way of caring for yourself. This does not mean you have to do whatever someone wants and keep them happy. Other's happiness is their own job, not yours'.

Lie 6: My needs and feelings are not as important as my parent's needs and feelings.

Truth: You are an amazing and valuable human being, and your needs and feelings are just as important as your anyone else's. You are doing the right thing when you take care of yourself, say no and set boundaries with situations that hurt your mental health.

Here are a few different exercises to use to convince your subconscious of these truths (pick 2).

1. Create affirmations from these truths (or use the list at the end of this chapter) and...
   - Write the affirmations out 10 times each whenever you feel guilty and first thing in the morning and right before bed. The reason is I say the last part is because whatever you put in your mind first thing in the morning tends to set the thought patterns for your day, and what you put in your mind before going to bed

tends to sink deep into your subconscious. So put these positive concepts in your mind first thing in the morning and lastly at night to keep your thoughts positive during the day, or...

- Say the affirmations to yourself (out loud if possible) first thing in the morning and right before bed or whenever you feel guilty or are having thoughts of guilt. As you say the truth/truths, *say it/them with conviction in your voice, as if you believe these truths right now!* To do this:
    o Use passion in your voice and speak dynamically like a mega church preacher or motivational speaker
    o Smile
    o Hug yourself or imagine hugging yourself
    o Use your hands as you speak

2. Spend a minute or two each day (morning or right before bed is best) visualizing yourself feeling like you entirely believe this new positive concept. As you do this, in your mind, bring the picture up close, make it big and life sized, and make it bright. See yourself standing or sitting somewhere

feeling this new concept is absolutely true. Feel that feeling.

3. Try a coach or therapist who uses hypnosis or hypnotic techniques. Most therapists and coaches help clients by changing their conscious thoughts. But experts says 95% of our feelings come from the beliefs in the unconscious mind, while only 5% come from our conscious thoughts. Over time, changing your conscious thoughts can create change at the unconscious level, but it takes a really long time (from my own experiences and many clients I have worked with). Unlike standard therapy or coaching, hypnosis, or hypnotic techniques such as NLP, EMDR, brainspotting and other methods, create change at the unconscious level and create results much faster. If you're interested in trying hypnosis or hypnotic coaching specialized in toxic family recovery, <u>click here to find out more about working with me.</u>

Affirmations for eliminating guilt:

☐ I believe setting boundaries is healthy

☐ I believe setting boundaries is an act of self-defense

☐ I believe setting boundaries is noble and virtuous

☐ I believe setting boundaries makes me a more loving person

☐ I believe saying no is healthy

☐ I believe saying no is noble and virtuous

☐ I believe saying no makes me a more loving person

☐ I believe others are responsible for their feelings, not me

☐ I believe disrespectful, controlling, and devaluing behaviors towards me is wrong

☐ I believe people that hurt me, mistreat me or disrespect me deserve boundaries

☐ I believe I deserve basic respect, and anything less is wrong.

☐ I believe my needs, feelings and emotional well-being is just as important as others

☐ I believe my needs, feelings and emotional well-being *is worthy of protection and care*

CHAPTER 14:
WHEN AND HOW TO REBUILD RELATIONSHIP

So you have gone no contact with a parent, and now they are wanting to reconcile. How do we know if we should give a parent that has been toxic another chance for relationship? The best answer to that is to find if they have changed. And that's where things get tricky. If am completely honest with you, in most cases toxic parents do not change. Their pride and ego are so strong, and they normally have so enablers around them that help them stay comfortable with their toxic patterns and do not change. However, though at least a little more unlikely than likely, it is still possible.

Here are some things to look for to tell if a previously toxic parent has changed.

- How much time has gone by? Has it been just a few months (which means it less likely)? Or has it been a few or several years (more likely)?

- Have they apologized and owned up to what they did? Or did they just come at you with excuses? Or avoid talking about the boundaries you set or hurt they caused?
- Have they said they now will agree to respect your boundaries?
- What steps have they taken in their life to change their behavior? Counseling, small groups, support groups, medication, etc.

The more of these things you can check off, the more likely it is they have changed.

Another thing to ask yourself ask is, are you ready? Are you in a place emotionally, where you can deal with this parent if they haven't changed? If they start disrespecting you, trying to manipulate, control, guilt trip, or abuse you again, how much would that affect you? If you aren't ready for that, guess what; its ok. *It's completely ok to put them off if you aren't ready and wait until you are* if you ever are. You might think, "well what if they have changed and I don't give them a chance?" Chances are they haven't changed. They might have, but the odds are not in their favor. It's not worth the risk if you aren't ready to deal with them. They probably had plenty of chances before you went no contact with them, you do not owe them another chance. If you want to give them a chance and you are emotionally ready to do that, great! But you are not obligated to.

If you decide to begin to restart a relationship with a toxic parent, the best thing you can do is *start slowly*. <u>You have to take it slow</u>. Think of what it's like getting into a freshly drawn bath, if you just jump right in, there's a chance it will be too hot, and you will get hurt. Instead you take it slow. You put in one toe, or a foot. Then if it's ok, you put in another foot. Then if that's ok, you slowly sit down, and then lean back into the tub. But if at any point it's too hot, you get, out and you wait a while longer until it cools down. *Same with restarting a relationship with parent that has a history of being toxic.* If you just jump right in, chances are you're going to get hurt. You take it slow, both with the amount of time, and the platform where you communicate. The chances are much lower you're going to get sucked in or hurt again.

Some practical ways to do this are:

- Start out with digital contact rather than face to face. I highly suggest emailing or using a video message app like with the Marco Polo.
- Only contact them once a month or every few weeks. If things are going well, you can increase the frequency, and maybe meet the

for coffee or lunch. If that goes for a while, then maybe have dinner together at your home

The ultimate test.

What is ultimately going to let you know if the parent is ready for a relationship or not is how they handle boundaries and you bringing up issues and being told no. At some point, you want to try saying no to something and communicating an issue, whether in the past or present, and see how they handle it. Don't try to make it easy on this parent. Don't purposefully make it hard, but don't try to protect them from unpleasant situations like being told no or having a boundary set. This is what is going to tell you if they can be trusted or not, or if they're pretending to be nice temporarily until they have manipulated you back into a relationship where they have control over you. You want to know as soon as possible if they are ready for relationship, because you don't want to open your heart to someone and then find out that they're the same as they were and now they've created more hurt. So don't avoid the tough conversations, set a boundary and say no as soon as possible before you get too emotionally involved.

SECTION 4
HEALING EMOTIONAL TRAUMA

CHAPTER 15:
STOP NEEDING YOUR PARENT'S APPROVAL

I have seen many people that continue to struggle with low self-worth and are very overly sensitive to what their parents say and do, and their toxic parent's treatment continue to cripple them, even after going no contact. *This is because they are still looking for their parent's approval and validation.* It is ok to enjoy our parent's love, and desire it, but when we need it and depend on it for our sense of worth, belonging and love, we are handicapping ourselves emotionally. When we continue to seek validation and approval from a normal or somewhat healthy parent, our self-worth will be shaky at best, if we do this with a narcissistic parent, we will be broken for the rest of our lives. As long as we NEED their approval or validation, they have power over our happiness, and self-worth. When we don't need our parent's approval to feel valuable, lovable, and worthy, and can love and value ourselves no matter what they think, the poor ways they treated us hurt MUCH less, we are much less sensitive to how they treat us today, and we will find it is much easier to grow our self-esteem and self-worth. Although this is not the case with everyone, and I do not recommend anyone be around someone who is emotionally abusive. Many adult children who are able to let go of needing their parent's affirmation find that they are able to have somewhat of a relationship with their parents and simply set and enforce boundaries whenever there is an unwanted behavior, rather than feeling triggered and running away. Here's how to stop needing your parent's approval (see the end of this book for all the affirmations):

Let go of the expectation for your parent's love or approval.

If you have toxic parents, it is unlikely you will ever get their unconditional love or approval. Any affection you get from them will be short-lived or have a self-seeking motivation. Expect that they will never give you the love and approval you deserve. It's important you come to this realization now, grieve and move on rather than spending the rest of your life grieving. Do what you need to in order to let this go. Have a pretend funeral, write down your expectations on a note, tie it to a balloon and let it go, or write a letter telling your parent you release them from the expectation to give you the love you deserve. This will not only help you feel less hurt, but it will also help you have less anger towards your parents. It's much easier to not be mad at someone or feel hurt by them when you aren't expecting anything from them and don't NEED anything from them.

Affirmation:

☐ "Although my parents will never give me the love and approval I need, I can and will find it somewhere else."

Knock them off of the pedestal.

Toxic parents make their children think they are far above them in importance and value. Unfortunately, many adult children do not realize this and do not consciously change how they see their parents. When we have deeply engrained beliefs that our parents are much more important than us, we value their opinion of us too highly. When they don't like us or love us, it is crushing, because a very important person has disapproved of us. Learn to see your parent's as just people who you are equal to in importance.

Affirmations:

- "I believe my parents are just people like me"
- "I believe I am just as important and valuable as my parents"

Realize your parents aren't right about everything.

Toxic parents instill in their kids that they are right about everything. And so often without realizing it, many adult children with toxic parents feel that their opinions are always right even if they hate the parent or parents. They may not admit that they value the opinion of this parent they hate so much, but they are still triggered and angered by the parent's disapproval. And it's because this adult child still has a deeply engrained, unconscious belief that whatever mom or dad thinks is gospel truth. The key is to realize your parents are imperfect in their thinking. They are capable and guilty of faulty thinking from time to time, especially when it comes to your worth and value.

Affirmations:

☐ "I believe my parents opinion of me is flawed"

Realize their disapproval of you is a "THEM" problem, not a "you" problem.

If a parent is mad at you, doesn't like you, or doesn't approve of you, this does not mean you are unlovable, bad or unworthy, this means they have issues. It speaks of their faulty thinking, not your worth. Your flaws are normal and do not take away form how lovable and valuable you are. And if the reason your parents aren't happy with you or don't like you is because you won't let them control you, that is because of their selfishness, not you.

Affirmation:

☐ "I believe my parent's disapproval of me is because of THEIR faulty thinking and THEIR issues"

Focus on what the good people in your life think of you.

Chances are there are many people in your life that love and appreciate you. If this is not the case, I would challenge you to get out and meet more people. Join a club or gathering of some sort where people have similar interests or values. Even finding a caring therapist can help you see your value. This will provide your subconscious with evidence that your parent's opinion is not the right one.

Affirmation:

☐ "I believe it's ok if my parents don't approve of me, because there are many people that do."

Build your self-worth and love.

The more you build up your self-worth and self-love, the less your parent's disapproval, anger or disappointment will hurt you. The less you will

NEED them. We will talk about building self-worth later, but for now know the best things you can do are keys for are:

1. Saying or writing affirmations first thing in the morning, before bed and as needed.
2. Visualization.
3. Self-care (practicing good hygiene, dressing more nicely, saving money to treat yourself to nice things once a month, meditation).
4. Talk therapy, or NLP/hypnosis.

Use power affirmations.

I talk about affirmations a few times in this book because they can be very powerful if you use them consistently, and in the right way. If we just say things it is not very affective, but if we say them with power, conviction, and enthusiasm (using dynamic tones of voice, using your hands, and smiling) we are telling our subconscious we believe these things and we will begin to believe them. I recommend you use affirmations first thing in the morning, right before bed, and as needed throughout the day. Here are the affirmations I pointed out throughout this chapter I suggest you use:

☐ "Although my parents will never give me the love and approval I need, I can and will find it somewhere else."

☐ "I believe my parents are just people like me"

☐ "I believe I am just as important and valuable as my parents"

☐ "I believe my parents opinion of me is wrong"

☐ "I believe my parent's disapproval of me is because of THEIR faulty thinking and THEIR issues."

☐ "I believe it's ok if my parents don't approve of me, because there are many people that do."

CHAPTER 16:
BUILDING YOUR SELF-WORTH AND LOVE

Toxic relationships primarily do three things: They make us feel powerless; they make us feel like our feelings and needs are worthless and important, and they take away our sense of value and worth if we had any to begin with. We reclaim our sense of power when we learn to set boundaries, but we must also build our sense of self-worth, sense of worthiness, and respect, and self-love to fully heal and become more resilient to toxic behavior.

I want to give you some actions to take to start loving yourself, and I want to share why many other tactics to loving yourself don't really work or work but are very, very slow. In case you're unaware there are two parts to your mind. The conscious and the subconscious mind. The conscious mind is responsible for logic, decisions making, problem solving, etc. That's the part of your mind you're using when you think thoughts. The subconscious mind is where your beliefs are held. Your beliefs are what decide how you feel. If you want to love yourself, you need to change the beliefs that are in your subconscious mind. A lot of different practices focused on loving yourself don't work very well or work very slowly, because they aren't geared to penetrate the subconscious mind, they are focused on the conscious mind.

Actions to build your self-worth and love:

- **Write down 10 things or qualities that you like about yourself.** When you do this, *be specific*. For example, if you believe you're a good spouse or partner, write down what makes you a good spouse or partner. Are you helpful? A good listener? Affectionate? Be specific as possible, this provides evidence for your subconscious mind to believe it. Then once the list is made, you want to read over it each day, either morning or before bed, or both. Whatever you put in your mind before bed, your subconscious will take that and keep thinking on it even as you sleep. Putting positive things in your mind before bed, is very powerful. As you read over each quality, smile. Try this for 10 seconds each quality.

- **Write down 3-5 positive things about yourself, whether good qualities or good things you have done that day or the day**

before. Smile at yourself as you write each one.

- **Do POWER affirmations:** Many of you might have already tried affirmations and felt like they weren't effective. Just saying affirmations mostly affects the conscious mind, but not the subconscious mind. But doing affirmations with smiling and enthusiastic/powerful tones of voice more powerfully affects your subconscious mind and emotions. This is going to super drive your affirmations. So when you say affirmations like "I love myself, I like myself, I'm amazing," try saying these with a smile and with power and conviction in your voice. "I LOVE myself!" "I think I'm absolutely AMAZING!"

- **Smile at yourself.** You may or may not realize it, but when you smile at others, you actually like them more. Whatever you smile at, you're going to like more and feel better about. So smile at yourself!! Try looking in a mirror and smiling for 10-15 seconds.

- **Use your skills or talents to help others or find a job where you can use them.** If you're a great cook, throw a dinner party and cook a 6-course meal, or go to culinary school and work at a restaurant. If you give great advice, create a Tik Tok or Youtube channel, and look into becoming a teacher or counselor. Using your talents and skills to help others helps you fully realize and experience how much value you offer others.

- **Giving yourself a hug.** Getting hugged by someone makes you feel loved, liked, and appreciated. It tells your subconscious that you are lovable, valuable and worthwhile. The same thing happens when you hug yourself! Try it out in the morning or whenever you feel down on yourself.

- **Talk to yourself like a good friend.** Do you have someone in your life that you really, really love and enjoy? A friend, child, spouse or partner? Someone you act really happy, enthusiastic, and loving with whenever you see? Or if you aren't very emotional and enthusiastic yourself, do you know someone more extroverted in your life that acts very happy and loving when they see you and is supportive and understanding when you make a mistake? Treat yourself like that. When you wake up in the morning, or when you are feeling down, look in the mirror and talk to yourself like someone you really love and are happy to see. Smile, wrap your arms around yourself tightly, and tell yourself "I'm so glad you're alive and you are the way you are! I love you so much!" When you mess up and make a mistake, talk to yourself as a good friend would: "It's ok, it's not that big of a deal, everyone makes mistakes. Don't worry about it. You're still awesome!"

- **Exercise.** Exercise not only releases feel good endorphins that make you feel better about yourself and life, but by exercising and caring for yourself, you're telling your subconscious mind that you value yourself, and that you are valuable, and your subconscious will start to believe the message. Not to mention, it is easier to feel good about your body the better you look. Find something you enjoy doing, and just do it 5-10 mins day. That's all it takes.

- **Get professional support:** It is very difficult for human being to make major changes to our lives on our own. Stats show that is very rare that people that attempt significant life changes do so successfully or long-term. The stats go WAY up when they have another person guiding, supporting and validating them. Having a counselor can be helpful with this process, although many counselors are more generalized and cannot help a great deal recovering from toxic relationships. I offer coaching specialized for people who have grown up in toxic environment. <u>Click here to find out more about getting coaching with me.</u>

DEALING WITH DISTORTED THINKING

What I mean by distorted thinking is these faulty or unrealistic filters or beliefs that we view ourselves and our performance through. Distorted thinking causes shame, and it stops us from appreciating the good things we do. You can do all the exercises I mentioned, but if you don't deal with the distorted thinking that cause us to dislike or hate ourselves, your self-worth will not grow, or its growth will be severely hindered.

I am going to go over some common negative filters that cause us to dislike or hate ourselves, and I am going to present some positive and realistic thinking you can use to challenge the distorted filters with. There are other filters than the one's I'm going to mention, but by far these negative filters or beliefs are the most common one's I see.

Distorted Thinking About Ourselves

1: It's not ok to have flaws or make mistakes.

You can tell if you believe this lie when you feel really bad about yourself whenever you mess up or do something less than desirable. As a kid your parents probably got mad, and made you feel that it is not tolerable to make mistakes or do anything wrong, as a way to discourage you from making those mistakes. Rather than just allowing you to suffer the consequences of your choices while providing nurturing and support, they made you feel like you were worthless or unlovable when you made a mistake.

How to challenge this thinking.

Realize that...

- Everyone makes mistakes. Everyone has flaws. It's unavoidable. Mistakes are normal.
- Most people can tolerate your mistakes and shortcomings. If someone can't tolerate your mistakes, it is because of their problems, not you.
- Although you make mistakes, you do a lot of good things too.

2: I should be better than what I am.

This happens when you have parents that have standards that are too high. Nothing is ever good enough. Now you have a hard time being happy with yourself because you feel you should be better than what you are. You should be more talented, more confident, more mature, more athletic, etc.

How to challenge this thinking.

Realize that...

- We can always be better. No one is perfect.
- Instead of focusing on how good you could or should be, focus on how good you are now.
  - Try saying this to yourself, "Yes I could be better, but I am good the way I am. I add value to others the way I am now!" I may not be a model, but I'm in good shape. I may not be the smartest person in the world, but I'm very smart.

3: Others are better than me.

Often this thinking comes from focusing on what others are better at. Because if we compared ourselves to others fairly, we would see that for the most part we are as good as everyone else, maybe a little more or less. But we tend to focus only on the areas that they are better at then us.

How to challenge this thinking.

Realize that...

- Everyone has strengths and weaknesses. There are people that are better than you are certain areas, but you are better than them at other areas.
- Realize that even though someone is better than you at a certain area, that doesn't mean you aren't good at that area. You are still good at it!

Distorted thinking about our performance.

1: If something I do isn't perfect or I make mistakes, it is no good.

Pretend that you made an amazing 3 course dinner for your family. Everybody loved it. But someone of the chicken went a little bit too crispy, but it was still good and everyone loved it. If you have this type of thinking, you would feel like the whole dinner was RUINED!!"

How do challenge this thinking.

Focus on the positive more than the negative. Even though you made one mistake, you did a great job! And everyone loved the dinner!

2: What I did should/could have been better.

Think of the same scenario with dinner again, but in this case you could have added just a little more salt to the mashed potatoes. But it was still a good dinner. If you have the "should/could have been better" dinner was ruined! And you're a horrible cook!

How to challenge this thinking:

- Focus more on the positive than the negative.
- Example (using the chicken dinner analogy): Look at what you did right, and how everyone loved the dinner. You could have had a bit more salt, sure. But you did a great job! And you're a great cook.

An Action Plan to Get Rid of The Distorted Thinking.

Now that you have hopefully seen the negative filters causing you to dislike yourself and slow your progress to valuing yourself, you need to have a plan of action to attack these negative filters. Being aware of them is not enough. Here are three things I suggest you do to begin to be rid of these distorted filters.

1. **Create a list of the negative qualities you have.** Your flaws or areas you feel you should be better at. Underneath each one, challenge the distorted thinking that causes you to feel bad about this.
2. **Keep these negative filters in mind as you write out and read over you list of good qualities, and good things you did**

for the day. If you find that when you read over your list or write things out, you don't feel really good about those things, or these negative thoughts come popping in, such as, I made I should be better, I didn't do that perfectly, I made mistake here, challenge those distorted filters by focusing on the good you did, rather than the bad or what you didn't do.

3. **Whenever you start to feel bad about yourself, pause and analyze your thinking.** What are you thinking at that moment that is causing you to feel bad? Are you being unaccepting towards a mistake or flaw? Are you comparing yourself to someone else? Whatever it is, identify the negative belief, and challenge it in that moment with the positive thinking we just went over. Say the truth or positive thoughts out loud to yourself if you can or write it down speaking to yourself in second person.

4. **Say the truths to challenge distorted thinking as affirmations every morning or night.**
   This is a great way to pre-emptively attack the distorted filters and minimize the negative and self-critical thoughts patterns you have throughout the day.

Try using the following or some of the following (whichever ones you need to believe) as affirmations:

- I believe it's ok if I make a mistake, because I do plenty of good things
- I believe it's ok if I have flaws, because I have plenty of good qualities
- Even though I could be better, I believe I'm still really good
- Even though there are others who are better at..., I believe I am still good at it!

AFFIRMATIONS FOR BUILDING YOUR SELF-WORTH AND LOVE

☐ I love myself

☐ I love the person I am - my personality and character.

☐ I love my body

☐ I love my face

☐ I believe I am infinitely lovable and valuable to God/The Universe

☐ I believe I'm lovable to many people just how I am

☐ I am proud of the spouse/partner I am (if applicable)

☐ I am proud of the mother/father/son/daughter I am

☐ I am proud of my accomplishments

☐ I am proud of my skills and abilities

☐ I believe I have much value and benefit to offer the world and those around me

☐ I fully accept my flaws and mistakes I've made

☐ I know I could be better, but I'm still awesome how I am

☐ I know I make mistakes, but I do many more good things

☐ I know I have flaws, but I have many more good things about me

CHAPTER 17:
BUILDING SELF-RESPECT

Part of self-worth isn't just realizing the value you offer others, or how much you love yourself, but a major part is respecting yourself. Respecting yourself looks like valuing and caring for your feelings, needs, and wants. Toxic parents teach us when we are young that our feelings and needs don't matter or come second to everyone else. The best way to undo this belief and see your feelings, needs and wants are valuable, is to start acting and treating yourself like your feelings and needs matter. As you do this, you will notice others around your value will treat you the same way. Here some important steps to take to start doing this.

- **Set boundaries and say no:** I know we talked about this earlier, but I want to touch on another reason this is important. By setting boundaries and protecting yourself from disrespect and saying no and conserving your time, energy or resources, you are you are telling your subconscious mind that you are important and worth protecting.

- **Speak up for yourself:** If you are feeling hurt about something, if the steak you ordered medium rare comes to you well-done, say something. Don't remain quite to avoid conflict.

- **Ask for things you want or need:** A great way to build up the courage to do this is to practice with small things. If you're at a restaurant, ask the waitress or waiter for a side of ketchup or ranch, even if you don't really want it. Ask your coworker to borrow a pen. Ask your spouse to get you a drink from the kitchen. Don't overdo it and annoy people, try setting a goal to ask for just one thing a day. Asking for things tells your subconscious that your wants are important.

- **Pamper yourself:** Once in a while go to a spa, get your nails done, buy yourself an expensive steak, buy a nice pair of shoes, a dress or a suit. Have a treat yourself day like Donna and Tom from the sitcom "Parks and Recreation." Treating yourself well to nice things will tell your subconscious that you are valuable. I know this can be pricey, and you don't want to do this all time. So what you are going to do is save up for a "treat yourself" day or item. Put aside 5% of your income into a jar, and then at the end of the month, spend it all on something expensive for yourself. You might find when you do this, that you have been spending a lot of your money on cheap things you do not need. It is much better for your self-worth to save your money and spend it on one or a few expensive things for yourself from time to time, than buy a bunch of cheap crappy things.

- **Power affirmations:** As I said earlier, normal affirmations are simply just saying something, but with power affirmations you are using your body and tone of voice, which is much more powerful at effecting the beliefs in your subconscious mind than simply saying words. Use the affirmations below or tweak them to your liking.

AFFIRMATIONS FOR SELF-RESPECT AND SENSE OF WORTHINESS

☐ I believe disrespectful, controlling, and devaluing behaviors toward me are wrong and evil

☐ I believe I deserve love and basic respect

☐ I believe my needs, feelings and emotional well-being is just as important as other's

☐ I believe my needs, feelings and emotional well-being *is worthy of protection and care*

☐ I believe I deserve to be protected and safe

☐ I believe I deserve to have boundaries

☐ I believe I deserve to say no and conserve my time, energy and resources

☐ I believe my wants, needs and feelings deserve respect and care

WORK WITH MICAH

Do you have a situation you need expert 1 on 1 guidance on? Or are you held back from setting the boundaries you need to because of guilt, fear, obligation, or low self-worth?

I have 1:1 coaching available where I can help you make a personalized plan to deal with your situation with toxic family, or heal from emotional abuse.

If you are interested in working with me, type in the url into your search engine, and follow the directions.

https://linktr.ee/micahstephenscoaching

Best wishes,

Micah

Printed in Great Britain
by Amazon